The
WONDERFUL
PEN of
MAY SWENSON

May Swenson, of whom a fellow poet said, "May is clear-eyed, inventive, deeply American, high-spirited. Her achievement is enormous, luminous, and generous."

7/94

The WONDERFUL PEN of MAY SWENSON

R. R. KNUDSON

MACMILLAN PUBLISHING COMPANY
New York

MAXWELL MACMILLAN CANADA
Toronto

MAXWELL MACMILLAN INTERNATIONAL
New York   Oxford   Singapore   Sydney

Several poems previously appeared in the following publications: "My Poems" in *The Nation;* "I'm One" from "The Rest of My Life" in *Poetry;* "Nightly Vision" in *The Raven Anthology;* "Haymaking" in *The Saturday Review of Literature.*

"Come In Go Out" and "If I Had Children" previously appeared in *In Other Words* by May Swenson. Reprinted by permission of Alfred A. Knopf, Inc.

"The Key to Everything" and "Mornings Innocent" previously appeared in *The Love Poems of May Swenson* by May Swenson. Reprinted by permission of Houghton Mifflin Company.

"A Boy Looking at Big David," "By Morning," "The Centaur," "Feel Like a Bird," "Fountains of Aix," "Her Management," "Living Tenderly," "Question," "Southbound on the Freeway," "To Make a Play," and "The Wonderful Pen" previously appeared in *The Complete Poems to Solve* by May Swenson and published by Macmillan Publishing Company.

"The Exchange," "The Garden of St. John's," "Horses in Central Park," "I Will Lie Down," "The Poplar's Shadow," "Sun," and "Zambesi and Ranee" were published previously in *New & Selected Things Taking Place* by May Swenson. Published by Atlantic/Little, Brown & Co.

The following poems are published here for the first time: "Alone in the House," "Golden Anniversary," "I Wish I Were Covered with Fur," "Oh, to Be a Tigress!" "Theatre Piece II," "Thursday Thoughts of a Poet," and "The Truth Is Forced."

"Good Lord" by Anca Vrbovska is used with permission of her literary estate.

First edition
Printed in the United States of America

10   9   8   7   6   5   4   3   2   1

The text of this book is set in 12 point ITC Garamond Lite.

Library of Congress Cataloging-in-Publication Data
Knudson, R. Rozanne, date.
    The wonderful pen of May Swenson / R.R. Knudson. — 1st ed.
       p.   cm.
    Includes bibliographical references and index.
    Summary:–A biography of the American poet with excerpts from her poems and photographs from her personal collection.
      ISBN 0-02-750915-X
    1.–Swenson, May—Biography—Juvenile literature.   2.–Poets, American—20th century—Biography—Juvenile literature. [1.–Swenson, May. 2.–Poets, American.]
    I.–Title.
PS3537.W4786Z73 1993   811'.54—dc20   [B]   93-637

In loving memory
of Margaret and Dan Arthur Swenson,
May's mother and father

CONTENTS

THE WONDERFUL PEN

I invented a wonderful pen. Not a typewriter . . . I wanted to use
just one hand, the right. With my hand always bent, the ink tube
a vein in my wrist, fixed between finger and thumb the pen wrote
as fast as I could feel. It chose all the right words for my feelings.
But then, my feelings ran out through the pen. It went dry. I had
a book of wonderful feelings, but my right hand was paralyzed.
I threw away the pen.

I invented a dream camera: a box, with a visor or mask . . . like a
stereopticon. When I awoke, I could view, and review, my dreams,
entire, in their depth. Events, visions, symbols, colors without
names, dazzled, obsessed me. They scalded my sight, I threw
away the camera. I had a moving picture of my wonderful dreams,
but I was blind.

So with my left hand I wrote, I had been lazy so long . . .
The letters went backwards across the page. Sometimes they went
upside down: a "q" for a "b," a "d" for a "p," or an "n" for a "u,"
and "m" for a "w." And it got worse. Now, since I can't read, or
see, not even the mirror can tell me, what I mean by the first
line by the time I've written the last line. But my feelings
are back, and my dreams . . .

What I write is so hard to write. It must be hard to read.
So slow . . . So swift my mind, so stupid my pen. I think I'll invent
a typewriter . . . For the left hand, and no eyes. No! I throw
away the thought. But I have a wonderful mind: Inventive. It is
for you to find. Read me. Read my mind.

—MAY SWENSON

1
LIVING TENDERLY

young girl sits on the floor turning pages of a book. She wears a white dress and white socks. Her mother and father sit behind her on the couch. Their legs encase her, making her feel warm and snug. Her name is Anna Thilda May Swenson, called May for the month of May.

She loves her soft book made of cloth. She feels the smooth pages between her thumbs and forefingers. She turns to a picture of a huge elephant. The trunk is raised, the tip of it facing May. The nostrils seem like eyes looking at her. She thinks about the trunk that's a nose. There are words in a row under the elephant that May can't read. She's so young she can't even walk yet. But she sees the elephant clearly. Seeing this elephant is her first memory.

"I know everything by looking," May said about herself years later.

By then she'd become *the* May Swenson, a famous poet. Thousands of children had read her poems in their schoolbooks. College students studied May in classes. Poetry lovers found May's latest poems printed in their favorite magazines. Her fellow poets, some of them as famous as May, wrote to her to say they admired her work. And she'd won prizes and grants and fellowships, lots of them.

May Swenson as a young child. The chair she is standing on was made by her father, an accomplished carpenter.

May welcomed fame. One reason she had been writing all her life was to be noticed by readers. She especially enjoyed the praise of other poets. If anyone knew what poetry was all about, they did.

Just as welcome to May as fame was the money she had made from writing poems. She'd set out in life to be a full-time, professional writer. She wanted to work for herself and for no one else. By living simply, frugally, and by writing poems good enough to sell to publishers and then win awards, May had achieved her goal.

What's more, she'd done it by "living tenderly." She'd stayed aloof from the gossipy world of writers. She'd made few enemies in the cutthroat business of getting published. Shy and quiet, she'd won friends by being steady and dependable and keeping her word, and by helping others with their writing projects.

May's poem about a turtle, "Living Tenderly," describes the quiet, inward, independent life she lived.

LIVING TENDERLY

My body a rounded stone
with a pattern of smooth seams.
My head a short snake,
retractive, projective.
My legs come out of their sleeves
or shrink within,
and so does my chin.
My eyelids are quick clamps.

My back is my roof.
I am always at home.
I travel where my house walks.
It is a smooth stone.
It floats within the lake,
or rests in the dust.
My flesh lives tenderly
inside its bone.

2

ALONE IN
THE HOUSE

*M*ay was born on May 28, 1913, in the small mountain town of Logan, Utah. She was the first child of Margaret and Dan Arthur Swenson. Her parents had come to live in Utah from their native Sweden.

Dan Swenson earned his family's living by teaching woodworking at Utah State Agricultural College in Logan. He was a wonderful carpenter. He made May a rocking horse and a rocking chair. He made her a wooden wheel on a stick to push as she ran. When she got tired of running, he'd push May smoothly around the yard in a cart he'd built in his shop. He played horse and bear with May, riding her on his shoulders. May grabbed handfuls of his hair for the reins. He roared and whinnied when May asked him to.

"Dad showed me the moon. He told me its name with a kiss in my ear. He showed me the sun and his garden and fruit trees," May said about her first playmate.

Soon May had three brothers to play with: Roy, born when May was two years old; Dan, born when she was three; George, born in 1917 when May was four.

They played lion under the dining-room table that their dad had built from yellow-grained wood. They made tents on the back lawn from clean sheets their

Above: *May's father shows her off near the rented house where she was born—445 North Seventh Street East, Logan, Utah.*
Below: *May in her sash and bow, with her mother holding baby George. Brothers Dan and Roy look on.*

mother hung on the clotheslines, pinning the sheets to the ground with nails from their dad's toolbox. They played marbles and jacks. They had penknives to flip into the grass for their games of mumblety-peg.

This crew of children rarely came inside in summer—only for lunches and suppers of fresh peas, beans, carrots, tomatoes, and other vegetables from their dad's garden and for cherries, apricots, peaches, and pears from the orchard. May ate thousands of green gooseberries. She loved their sour flavor and the way they popped between her teeth. She'd gather flowers in a bowl, add cold water, and feed them to herself for fun. Once she nearly swallowed a bee.

In the fall there were apples for sauce, for pies, and for juice. In winter the children all ate smoking bowls of oatmeal for breakfast, to make them "grow taller," their dad promised them. He served them honey from the beehives he kept in the backyard.

After meals there were dishes to wash—dishes, pans, kettles, and more dishes. The boys went off to stack wood for the water heater. They weeded the garden and picked strawberries and raspberries. May helped with the dishes. She could reach the low kitchen sink without standing on a stool. While the water heated, May planned her getaway from housework. She'd slip out and run to a nearby hay field. She'd made paths through the hay and a cave in it.

There she'd lean against a fence pole. She'd take a book from a table of hay and look at the pictures. She kept the Oz books and *Alice in Wonderland* in her cave. When her mother called from the house, May pretended not to hear.

Every afternoon for one whole summer May would run to the new house her dad was building for his family. The tops of the cement basement walls were cool for sitting. But May didn't sit for long. She'd given herself the task of jumping from a high wall to the dirt floor. She was frightened by the height. She always began her jump by thinking, I can't do it. No. Yes. No. Yes, I will. I have to jump now. Now!

She'd jump and feel strange and wild and powerful. To May, power was fear pushed back. The power of fear would carry her anywhere, as high as she liked. Her bare toe prints in the dirt were a secret sign she'd turned her fear inside out.

"Mother says go home and do the dishes. The water's hot," May's brothers would yell from the top of the walls.

Then the three boys would tumble into the dirt, landing easily, sloppily. They'd climb the half-finished basement steps and jump again. May noticed they didn't seem to "feel anything" about their jumps.

New walls rose slowly from the ground on North Fifth Street in Logan. May's father had to spend most of the day teaching his students how to use tools for building. After that he'd walk down College Hill to the new house and work on it. People around the neighborhood called it the White House because of the white stucco walls above the basement. Neighbors were impressed with the three floors and many rooms. Some of these rooms would be rented to help repay the loans that built the house.

The house was a short walk from May's school, Webster Elementary. She went off to first grade speaking only Swedish. She'd spoken Swedish at home and during visits with her grandparents, uncles, aunts, and cousins in Utah. So May was surprised and puzzled by the English words flying around the classroom. But she quickly fell in love with the schoolbooks, with the smell of them, and with their glossy pictures. She learned to speak and read English perfectly.

May walked to school and to the Logan library, even in cold Utah winters. She wouldn't have minded the cold if she'd been better dressed for it—dressed like the boys in her neighborhood. They wore sturdy jackets, aviator caps, and mittens, all made of leather. They raced on the ice of the irrigation canal while May shuffled and stumbled along on the canal's bank. Her dress was too long and loose. Her rubber boots were too large. She worried that she'd fall down and scrape her knees.

She'd fallen many times. Other children had laughed at her. Three boys had rushed at her with snowballs to poke down her coat. When she saw them she tried to slip past. She tried to make herself invisible.

Did her clothes make her a girl? May asked herself that many times. Or was it because she happened to be a girl that she must wear the flimsy clothes that caused her to feel awkward and slow?

I can't run away or fight back, May thought. I wish I were covered with fur like an animal. Then I'd dare go anywhere.

I wouldn't have to worry
I'd be so warm and furry
I wouldn't care
If people stare

May wrote that little poem years later when she remembered her feelings of being an ill-dressed, clumsy child who wasn't expected to fight back like her brothers.

Roy and Dan didn't have to worry about the bullies who chased them in Logan. They made short work of the German kids who picked on the Swedes. The Swenson brothers got their dad to give them a switch to use. They hid in some bushes, then jumped out and waved the switch menacingly until the "Berliners" gave up.

May turned inward to solve her problems. She'd escape to the garden or orchard to read and think. She'd listen to the whirring bees and to the neighbor's horses. May loved to be alone, away from the larger and larger Swenson family.

May's family belonged to the Mormon church, and her mother, especially, spent much of her time doing church work. She helped gather and cook food for poor Mormon families. She helped take care of Mormons who were sick. She never missed Sunday school and other church meetings. She sang in the choir.

Above all she was humble and kind and tender. She tried with all her heart to help her children believe in a Heavenly Father. She asked them over and over to obey God's laws. If they were good Mormons they would be together as a family in heaven, she believed, as other Mormons did. She worried about May. May was a child who believed what she saw with her own eyes. The Mormon religion, based on an unseen God in an unseen heaven, was going to be hard for May to swallow.

The birth of May's three sisters—Grace in 1921, Ruth in 1922, and Beth in 1923—meant even more housework for May and her mother to do: floors to sweep and scrub more often, endless dishes to wash, wipe, and put away. May also helped with the cooking and baking. She learned to iron her brothers' shirts and to do the laundry. For that she could be alone in the

Margaret Swenson emigrated from Sweden to Utah, there to raise nine children. In 1923 these were seven (below, left to right): George, Ruth, May, Grace, Roy, Beth, and Dan. Years of housework and child care did not spoil Margaret's love of family. She helped with her many grandchildren, who often stayed with her in Logan.

May praised her kind and gentle mother in the poem "Her Hands."

basement. She could read in the times between taking the clean clothes from the washing machine, changing the water, and putting dirty clothes in. She would sit and stare at the furnace, at the dancing orange flames behind the vents. She liked the smell of soapy water going down the drain in the smooth cement floor. She liked to listen to sounds other than human voices: the snap of logs in the grate; the swirl of water; and a mouse in the house.

ALONE IN THE HOUSE

I heard a little noise, not my own,
not inside my head but inside my house.

Like a tooth testing a tiny bone.
It must, I thought, be a mouse. . . .

So I listened to silence for a full minute.
What a large place it is, what depth is in it! . . .

Please, little mouse, make your scratch.
Munch, scamper—I promise not to catch.

Any little noise is better, less scary
than a house full of nothing, dark, huge, hairy!

After her chores, May had a chance to play with her friend Muriel, who lived next door. They would make plans by leaving notes for each other in a cigar box high in an apple tree. Muriel was left-handed. May was fascinated by that. Muriel's handwriting was an odd, plump backhand, different from May's small, exact letters.

Lying in bed each morning, May was filled with suspense. She'd think about the message waiting for her, knowing there was one because she'd watched Muriel climb the tree to leave it.

May would jump from bed, run through the wet grass, through the corn patch, to the apple tree. She'd pull herself from branch to branch. She'd feel the crisp leaves and apples bumping her face. She'd lift the cigar-box lid to find a folded note, written on paper that May had given to Muriel for her birthday.

One note from Muriel, which May saved all her life, was in dark blue ink. Its corners were curled with dew.

Dear MS—Francis and I we will call for you at 3.30 by the gat an go to her hous to mak her brother let us rid the Bike. Anser emediately. Your best Frend.

M. M.

The summer May was ten she'd go out "riding" every day. She wrote about her imaginary horse, Rob Roy, in her poem "The Centaur." "The Centaur" shows May's love for horses. It also reveals her belief that she was part animal herself. But that's not all we find out from this poem about riding. At the end of it, May tells of her mother's disapproval of the centaur—May—running wild.

The summer that I was ten—
Can it be there was only one
summer that I was ten? It must

have been a long one then—
each day I'd go out to choose
a fresh horse from my stable

which was a willow grove
down by the old canal.
I'd go on my two bare feet.

But when, with my brother's jack-knife,
I had cut me a long limber horse
with a good thick knob for a head,

and peeled him slick and clean
except a few leaves for the tail,
and cinched my brother's belt

around his head for a rein,
I'd straddle and canter him fast
up the grass bank to the path,

trot along in the lovely dust
that talcumed over his hoofs,
hiding my toes, and turning

his feet to swift half-moons.
The willow knob with the strap
jouncing between my thighs

was the pommel and yet the poll
of my nickering pony's head.
My head and my neck were mine,

yet they were shaped like a horse.
My hair flopped to the side
like the mane of a horse in the wind.

My forelock swung in my eyes,
my neck arched and I snorted.
I shied and skittered and reared,

stopped and raised my knees,
pawed at the ground and quivered.
My teeth bared as we wheeled

and swished through the dust again.
I was the horse and the rider,
and the leather I slapped to his rump

spanked my own behind.
Doubled, my two hoofs beat
a gallop along the bank,

the wind twanged in my mane,
my mouth squared to the bit.
And yet I sat on my steed

quiet, negligent riding,
my toes standing the stirrups,
my thighs hugging his ribs.

At a walk we drew up to the porch.
I tethered him to a paling.
Dismounting, I smoothed my skirt

and entered the dusky hall.
My feet on the clean linoleum
left ghostly toes in the hall.

Where have you been? said my mother.
Been riding, I said from the sink,
and filled me a glass of water.

What's that in your pocket? she said.
Just my knife. It weighted my pocket
and stretched my dress awry.

Go tie back your hair, said my mother,
and *Why is your mouth all green?*
*Rob Roy, he pulled some clover
as we crossed the field,* I told her.

3

QUESTION

*M*ay's cousin Edna—nicknamed Sunny— was the first to name May a poet.

Sunny used to visit and play paper dolls with May. They'd cut models from the Sears catalog and cut out extra clothes to fit them. One day when they were playing, May showed a page of her diary to Sunny. May had typed the page with two fingers on her dad's typewriter.

"You've written a poem," Sunny exclaimed, looking at the short lines on the page. Sunny read the page aloud, and May recognized the kind of rhythm she'd heard when her teachers read poems at school.

May had been writing in her diary at a desk her dad had built for her. It had cubbyholes and small drawers. May didn't write things like "Dear Diary, Today I fed a squirrel." Instead she told about what was happening inside herself. On paper she'd discuss with herself the loneliness she felt despite living in such a big family. She'd write about her timidness and how hard it was for her to make friends at school. She felt she was different from other girls her age. She wrote about that.

"I wrote to amuse myself," May once said about her first diaries. Probably she wrote also to understand herself.

She also did her homework at her little cherry-wood desk. She received A's in most subjects. She won a scholarship pin in elementary school, and on one of her report cards her teacher wrote, "Anna May is a splendid student." On another report card the same teacher wrote directly to May: "You have been blessed with good parents, a real home, and I hope you will do something fine in the world."

May's brothers were less interested in reading and writing than she was, and they were much more active. They'd sit on the bumper of a bus until it got going fast, then they'd leap off, whooping. They'd ride their sleds down College Hill, weaving among cars in the snow, jumping an icy sidewalk and flying through the air. They had a police dog they tried to hitch to their sleds. May named him Cop.

She would go with her brothers to hoe weeds in a neighbor's vegetable patch. Before finishing, they'd sneak away to take dips in the canal. May went into the water only up to her waist. No further! She hadn't learned to swim and she was scared.

When the circus came to the Logan fairground the Swenson children got to go as a reward for doing their jobs around the house and garden. They went to parades on the Fourth of July and again on the twenty-fourth of July, this time to celebrate the Mormons' first settlement in Utah in 1847. Picnics on the college lawns were also fun for the Swensons. They'd all walk up College Hill together. "Climbing the hill prepares you for effort; the physical sparks the mental climb," said May's dad.

A special treat for the children one year was a ride in an airplane. Their dad paid fifteen dollars to the pilot of a Ford trimotor to take them up for fifteen

The Swensons, 1925. May and George wear sailor blouses, in fashion then for boys and girls. Later May wrote about her brothers: "All those white shirts! I had to iron them."

minutes. They flew over the farms of Cache Valley. Their mother was weeping when they landed. She'd been afraid they'd crash.

The Swenson family would often visit relatives living south of Logan in Salt Lake City, Provo, and Pleasant Grove, Utah. The family took the train or drove the hundred miles or so. They stayed for a week or longer. Uncle Helge had a team of horses and May was always excited about riding them. She also loved to play cards at her uncle Warnick's house, shuffling the cards crisply and laying them out for a game of solitaire. May knew that Mormons believed that card playing was wrong. But she did it anyway. She was willing to be the black sheep of the family.

While visiting her grandpa Swenson, May earned a little money by swatting flies. Grandpa sat with his eyes closed. May dashed around the room with a flyswatter. He counted each strike.

"I got one," May called out. She looked forward to a penny for each of the five she'd already killed.

The room buzzed with flies, but they quickly rose out of May's reach. So she began swatting an empty wall to get richer. She made loud whacks, pretending she'd hit one. After a while she went to her grandpa for her pay.

With his eyes still closed he took a nickel from his vest pocket and gave it to her.

"Grandpa Swenson could tell from peoples' voices and from hesitations in their movements all he needed for seeing into the core of them," May later recalled.

She went south from Logan to Salt Lake again for her grandpa's funeral. There she lowered her head and cried like the people around her. She didn't know why. She didn't understand how final death was. Why were birds trilling and cheeping in the graveyard if death was so sad? May watched the coffin being covered with dirt. Everything would be spoiled, she thought. The wet dirt would get under the lid and onto the white cover—might even smear Grandpa, his clean face and brushed hair and beard.

May's curiosity about death continued the rest of her life. In her poems she often asked questions about what would become of *her* when she died.

QUESTION

Body my house
my horse my hound
what will I do
when you are fallen

Where will I sleep
How will I ride
What will I hunt

Where can I go
without my mount
all eager and quick
How will I know
in thicket ahead
is danger or treasure
when Body my good
bright dog is dead

How will it be
to lie in the sky
without roof or door
and wind for an eye

With cloud for shift
how will I hide?

May decided to use death as a way to conclude one of her first stories. In "Christmas Day" she writes about a boy who has a strange dream, wakes up, and hurries around the house to see what Santa has left him for Christmas. He's delighted by his costly gifts. Then he finds his mother and father dead. He's sad but not shocked. He accepts their deaths because of his dream, calmly saying: "They had gone to sleep for the last time."

For this story May won twenty-five dollars from *The*

Grizzley, her high-school newspaper. That was a large prize in those days.

As a teenager May sometimes gave way to angry, stubborn moods. She'd stamp her feet and howl. She'd lie on the floor, knees up to her chin, pretending to be a tree stump or a stone on the mountainside. She'd refuse to move or to speak.

Her dad would say, "May's just like her Aunt Marie." Aunt Marie was the odd, unpredictable member of the Swenson family.

But more often than not, May was the good, steady daughter, helping to lighten her mother's load. Her mother worked constantly. She'd be so tired by night that she'd have to soak her feet in a bucket of water. May did many chores around the house. She helped make root beer that the family drank in summers. She peeled fruit and boiled it in bottles to store in the basement. She tended her new baby sister, Margaret. There were eight Swenson children by the year 1928, when May was fifteen.

To get away from this mob, May would take some green apples and a salt shaker to the roof of a backyard shed. There she'd eat and write. One of her earliest wishes was to tell others about herself, but she was too shy to do it in person. As she grew older she'd write poems describing herself: "I am a thing that is like a disheveled wind," she wrote.

In this same poem May describes her friend Helen Richards: "You are the white stillness that lilacs wear after a warm rain," May wrote.

May and Helen were best friends for seven years. They went to school and church together. Helen was the sort of Mormon who didn't ask questions about life and religion. She believed what she was told. May questioned everything, for she was not shy with ideas. She noticed, for example, that the word *goodness* contains the word *God*. And *evil* is in the word *devil*. That made her think about where words came from. She knew words were made up by people. So people could also have made up the whole idea of God, heaven, and hell.

The Mormon religion seemed like superstition to May, but she didn't fuss about going to church meetings. She went with her parents, to please them.

It's not for me, she was thinking about religion— but not saying. She didn't want to hurt her sweet mother, who was worried about how different May was, compared to the other Swenson children and to the Swenson cousins. She wanted May to be more like the popular, outgoing Sunny.

"May wasn't like the rest of us girls," May's sister Grace once said. "We had fun brushing, combing, and arranging our hair. We tried on clothes and played dress-up. May wasn't like that. She'd frown at herself in the mirror as she braided buns to fit over her ears."

May hated to go shopping for clothes. For one thing there wasn't much money in a teacher's family. May was careful to ask for no more than her fair share for clothes. Also, she was uncomfortable around salesladies. Their smiles seemed fake to her. They seemed to be telling her lies about the skirts and dresses they urged her to buy. May thought it was silly to be pinched by tight clothes just to be in fashion. She'd rather be wearing her brothers' hand-me-downs.

Yet she wanted the approval of others in Logan High School. For that she'd have to conform, blend in, at least until college. She could be an animal—a tigress— only in her mind and poetry.

OH, TO BE A TIGRESS!

Oh, to be a tigress,
and wear the same costume
summer, winter, autumn, spring;
to slink into a room,
and hear the women all exclaim:
"How *chic* you look, my dear!"
Oh, not to have to give a darn
what's being worn this year! . . .

Necklines may plunge, hems rise or fall,
shoulders go square or round,
waists pinch in, hips plump out—
it matters not at all.
The tigress walks with perfect poise,
meets every fashion test,
because for all occasions
she's appropriately dressed.

And if she walks with special pride,
it rightfully is hers,
for who could hope to equal
such a gorgeous set of furs?

4

COME IN GO OUT

*A*t college May fell in with what her parents would have called the "wrong crowd."

May didn't have to leave Logan to do that. Starting in the fall of 1930 she walked right up College Hill every day to attend Utah State, where her dad had been teaching for years.

Her friends there were writers who got together to work on *The Scribble,* their college magazine. They read poems and stories sent to *Scribble* and chose which ones to publish. They read to one another from their own work, seeking one another's advice—and praise. They passed around books they were reading and talked about them excitedly. *Ulysses* by James Joyce was their favorite. Some called it "dirty." Some said it was the greatest novel they'd ever read. May was bowled over by it, by the fresh language and rhythm of the sentences.

May was known for her wise and original comments about books. She didn't quote what others said. She had her own ideas. She made up her mind and stuck to her decisions. A friend told her, "You're always so determined, headstrong, obstinate. And yet you're so sensitive."

May was also known for her kindly remarks about the writing of her classmates. One of them remembers,

"May would say, 'I like this, I like that.' She took our questions seriously. If we asked for help she would think up the precise words to express our ideas."

The Scribble published May's poems, the first magazine to do so. May also wrote articles for *Student Life,* the college newspaper. Her wit and wordplay often appeared in a regular column called "Hooey."

May's new friends drew her attention to politics in Utah. This was the time of the Great Depression. People needed jobs. May's friends claimed that Mormons were too powerful in Utah's government, that Mormons were stingy and just plain wrong about the way they ran Utah, that there should be a separation of church and state.

These same friends laughed at the Mormon rule against church members' smoking, and some of them smoked at *Scribble* meetings. They got May started smoking even though she knew her parents would be mad if they found out. At home May would sneak to the shed roof for a cigarette. She tried not to feel guilty. But at night, in her bad dreams, her parents found out and treated her coldly.

May had a new room at home. Her dad had closed in a porch, a space about twelve feet by fourteen feet, with a big window, a couch bed, and a slant-board desk for drawing and painting. May would pick flowers from her dad's garden, arrange them just so, and draw them. She'd hang her drawings on the walls. Then she'd notice how much more alive the flowers looked in their accidental arrangements in the garden.

She took classes in art. She drew sets for plays that were given in the college theater. She helped build scenery. As shy as May was, she went so far as to get up on stage and play a part in a silly comedy. That happened at the end of May's freshman year.

May did her best work for Dr. Pederson, a popular professor in the English department who taught creative writing. He liked May's stories so much that he asked her to read them aloud in class. He said he liked their "strength."

A classmate of May's recalls what May looked like when she was reading: "May read softly. Her blue eyes were filled with meaning. She was a short girl with brown silky hair that shined. She had small features. She wasn't pretty but she was beautiful."

Another classmate, Edith Welch, describes May as having a "beautiful animal face, with Slavic eyes—sympathetic eyes." Edith and May became best friends. They talked endlessly on the phone when they weren't together at chorus practice or at the theater working on sets.

Edith lived in Mendon, a farm community just outside Logan. Neither she nor May owned a car. May had never been taught to drive because her brothers handled the Swenson car. But one day May "stole" the car and steered it out through the hay fields to Mendon. May was nervous. The car's engine might die, for all she knew. She didn't get out from behind the wheel for her visit to Edith. They talked through the car's window. Then May turned the car around and drove home.

Their friendship deepened. "When I felt burdened I'd go to May," Edith remembers. "May would comfort me. She'd take the long view."

"Wait until tomorrow," May would say.

One day they walked up Logan Canyon for a picnic. May took along a bottle of maraschino cherries, Edith's favorite food. They cooked hamburgers over an open fire. They confided to each other that day. May said she

May and Edith Welch on campus, prepared for their hike along the river in Logan Canyon. Edith describes May as "chubby" during their college years together.

didn't care what others thought of her. She wasn't trying to be popular like some of the boy-crazy girls she knew. She didn't want to marry and raise a family. She said she could make her own way in the world.

"I may never be happy," May said, "because I can't have all of what I want. But there is respite in writing. If I can write, *if, if*."

For help in writing May played a game with herself. She'd sit at the typewriter and put down whatever popped into her mind. This automatic writing helped her get at the serious thoughts she'd then use in stories and poems:

> If I could write but i cant please let me write in a pink dress mrs. jenson but not poems fly and man on street tonight if i write and tragic life but not a good book will do anyway because i have nothing else to do powerful sunlight thru leaves go on go on never stop i wish many things but i am young am i not i am 20 years old in this summer i will grow older that is surely strange now i am already older and then you are dead perhaps death is like life only infinately more beautiful but am i happy now no i am wretched i wish and i am unfulfilled but when all is fulfilled theyre is nothing beyond and emptyness what then i don't know but i am glad i do not know.

Death was again on May's mind. Her new baby brother Lloyd had lived only eight months. At the funeral May saw her aunt Marie slip a gold watch into the coffin. The watch had been handed down in the Swenson family, and May was supposed to receive it when she was 21. May said nothing about her aunt's puzzling behavior. Growing up in a large family had

37

At Utah State May learned that others liked her writing.

perhaps helped May tolerate peoples' differences and even their unkind acts toward her.

At age 21, May graduated from Utah State with a bachelor of science degree. She marched in the ceremony with her dad in his professor's cap and gown.

"I'd had my little taste of glory," May said about her success as a writer in college. Now she wanted to find a larger audience for her writings.

She continued to live at home, working part time as a reporter for Logan's *Herald Journal,* hoping to become a full-time writer. Many of her friends had left town, but Edith Welch was still a student. She worked at a campus greenhouse in order to pay her room and board in Logan. May invited Edith to share the porch room, along with the Swenson cat, Tango.

"May and her family were good to me," Edith has said. "The only time I remember May being angry with me was when she read her poems in *Scribble* and found a mistake. It was *my* fault. I was editor the year after May was editor. What should have been 'bushes' came out 'brushes' on the page. May was a stickler for words. But after a while she decided that maybe 'mountain brushes' was better than 'mountain bushes.' "

Edith finished college and got married that next summer (1935). By then May had decided she'd outgrown Logan. "It's too pure and boring," she told friends. May didn't have the money or the daring to move farther than her uncle Ren's house in Salt Lake City. She stayed there with her cousin Sunny, who'd been taking dance classes for years, had won a dance contest, and now taught dance classes that were well attended. Sunny swept May up in a social whirl. May went to parties and out on dates with men Sunny introduced her to. May found herself an outgoing job—taking advertisements on the phone for the Salt Lake *Tribune*. She moved with ease around the Salt Lake valley on streetcars, buses, and trains.

May's moods went up and down, despite her new-found social life. Her moods can be followed in her Salt Lake diary:

"I made a good impression on myself, emphasizing my cleverness. . . . I'm restless. Time passes. I want glory. I'm broke. . . . I will come to nothing. . . . I haven't any fun. . . . I don't give two hoots for anything this week. . . . What is there to compare to this kind of joy?"

A plan began to form in May's mind, sparked by a friend from *Scribble* days, Gladys Hobbs. Gladys told May all about her trip to New York City, about the great plays and ballets and art galleries there. May had been longing to see the Georgia O'Keeffe paintings and the Alfred Stieglitz photographs she'd read about. May had also been reading novels by Thomas Wolfe. Wolfe lived in New York, as did hundreds of writers who'd moved there to have their work taken seriously by editors and readers. May wanted to be a New York City writer.

"I have been debating over and over whether to risk this no account carcus in N.Y.C.," May wrote in her diary. "I have no money. No pull. Nothing to grab in deep water. Have I the guts to put myself where I might starve?"

May's hopes of going to New York got a boost from Sunny. She was taking a bus to Pontiac, Michigan, to pick up a new car at the factory. Then she would drive on to New York for some fun. May was welcome to go along.

"It seems foolhardy," May told herself sternly.

She got up the nerve to ask her dad to lend her two hundred dollars. She said she wanted to "visit" New York. He agreed to the visit. May put the money in travelers' checks. She packed her clothes, stored her books and desk with Gladys, and took off. Her family thought she'd be back in Utah before long.

May and Sunny drove through farm country in Canada after they picked up the car. On a pad in her lap, May kept track of what she saw. "Men are pitching hay," she wrote to begin a poem, and continued, "By forkfuls they gather summer in, to heap in the cool barns":

> Snug against the rafters
> pile the yellow stuff of summer
> against the sun-crisp walls
> press the sweet grasses

Sunny and May stopped off in the mountains of New York to visit Sunny's tap-dance teacher. They went to see the Ted Shawn Dance Company in Massachusetts. Being up close to dancers made May feel "puny." She reminded herself she'd have to be "poised" in New York.

The night before she arrived, May wrote a letter to Thomas Wolfe. "Oh Thomas Wolfe," she began, "I shall come to your city—my CITY. I am coming into the thick of it. I crouch like a panther. A snarl meaning sweetness and rage rises in me."

With her soft voice, May couldn't have snarled if she'd tried! And her actions were too hesitant for pouncing. No, she'd simply arrive in New York City and quietly, in her careful way, she'd try to find a job. Then, in the years to come, she'd confess to the many moods of a writer, as in this poem comparing her inner struggle to nature's changeable weather.

The poem can be read down the page as well as across the page.

COME IN	GO OUT
A world of storm	A life of waves
Raging circles form	Tides and icy caves
Wind loops the globe	Sun scorching palms
Blizzards in the brain	Or deadening calms
Then modifying hope	A single summer day
A hoisted sail	Unfolds twinkling
On the dream trail	Flinches past the eye
Hummingbird's green	Bullet of gauze
Illuminant	Of primal cause

5

I'M ONE

*M*ay tried and tried to get a job on a newspaper in New York. When she couldn't she answered advertisements for "author's assistant."

The authors who May interviewed wanted to pay her a tiny salary to write their books from scratch. They asked May to sit at a typewriter, listen to their stories, and type them perfectly in her own words! May would be their ghostwriter.

She'd figured out she needed twenty dollars a week to live on. The authors weren't willing to pay that much. They believed May should be paid the wages of a typist, not a writer. May thought they were all "crackpots" for not trying to write their own stories. She gave up and put an ad of her own in the newspaper:

> "Writer, college degree, trained arts,
> literature. Keen, healthy, mental poise, age 23
> do anything progressive that nets money."

This ad brought May a job *and* a boyfriend. He hired May to help him write a play, and soon they were going to movies together, to art galleries, and out to dinner. May called him "Plat" in her diary. She wrote, "Plat's crazy about me. But I do not love. I want to. I'd rather love than be loved—tragedy rather than easy joy."

Work on their play went slowly. There was research for May to do, notes to take, trips to the library, and sheets of paper to be "splattered with words." May said she'd always thought writing a play would be brilliant business, but it wasn't, at least not with Plat in charge.

"It will be a long, long time before we can actually part the curtain and show the characters dressed for their parts," May grumbled to herself.

Her other grumbles were about money. Her clothes were wearing out and would have to be replaced. And Christmas was coming. May wanted to send presents home to Utah.

The holiday season of 1936 made May terribly home-sick. She'd been dreaming of the smell of her dad's pears. She missed her baby brother Paul, who'd been born only a year before she'd left Utah. May spent her rent money to mail gifts to everyone in her family. Her mother sent May a box of Swedish treats she cooked each year for Christmas dinner. In her letters she asked May to come home to Utah.

"Love is—home," May wrote in her diary.

Then she cheered herself up with "I'm a writer. I have my typewriter."

She also had a new job, a better one than with Plat, whose play never got produced. May now worked in an office on the thirty-fifth floor of Rockefeller Plaza. There she answered the phone, opened mail, and tried to help her boss write a book about the meaning of color. This job paid May enough to live on and a little extra for horseback riding every once in a while.

"I feel self-sufficient and independent on a horse," she wrote. "People get out of my way. My horse is alert, with pert ears." May later wrote a poem describing her favorite horses in Central Park:

This coal-colored stallion
flake of white on his brow
is slippery silk in the sun

Fox-red bay
and buckskin blond as wheat
Burgundy mare with tassled mane of jet

Somber chestnut burnished
by his sweat
to veined and glowing oak . . .

May didn't hold her office job for long. She made so many mistakes that her ears burned from being scolded. She predicted she'd be fired, and, when it happened, she gathered up her cigarettes and "made a noble exit." Now, with only thirty-nine dollars to her name, she called herself a "flop."

She wasn't really. She could have done well at office work if she'd tried. The truth was she had no desire to get ahead in the world of business. Instead she chose to be free, to be the "open eye" and to write about what she saw. She said, "There is such a hunger in me for beauty and the need to say it in my own words." May didn't want to work for other people.

Yet to keep from starving she had to find another job. This time she helped shorten a long autobiography and type it for a woman named Anzia Yezierska. May found the work fascinating because Anzia's story was about arriving in America from Poland and learning to earn a living by writing. Anzia had sold her stories to the movies in the past. She'd lived in Hollywood and been treated royally. But now she seemed to be as poor as May during the Great Depression. Anzia was slow to pay May the few dollars a week May needed for rent.

"People get out of
my way," May said
of riding.
Below, left: *In
Washington Square,
May shows off her
winter coat, bought
with relief money.*
Below, right:
*Anzia Yezierska
was moody but
helpful when May
worked as her typist
and editor.*

To save on rent, May moved downtown to Greenwich Village, where a room cost her only three dollars a week. It was furnished with a cot, a chair, a table, and a dresser. May's new boyfriend, Arnold, helped her move.

Arnold was Anzia's nephew. He had a car. On weekends he took May for rides in the country. He told May he liked her because she was honest.

"I think I shall be really honest with Arnold and see how he likes it," May threatened in the pages of her diary.

She went often to visit Arnold and borrow books from the shelves full of them in his large apartment. Together they read and discussed *Portrait of the Artist as a Young Man* by James Joyce. One evening she cooked dinner for Arnold, probably to show him she was grateful for his books. She was so nervous at the stove that she made a mess. A fork handle caught fire as she stirred the hash. The sardines she'd dug from a can made an oily heap on the serving plate. May's hair hung in her eyes the whole meal.

Not that she really wanted to excel as a cook! She'd rather discuss poetry and fiction and go to art galleries and ride to the ocean with Arnold. May had no thoughts of becoming a housewife, even though she was down to the last eighteen cents in her purse.

May's landlady told her to vacate the room. May went to Anzia for comfort. "Marry Arnold and you won't have to worry about a place to live," Anzia suggested.

"I won't marry him," May answered.

She loved her independence. Her coat was worn out. She didn't care. She had a big hole in one shoe but felt proud of it. Her 1937 Christmas package from Utah arrived at the shabby room she'd found to live in. Her mother's honey bread and *sylta* gave her energy to sit at her lopsided table and type her latest poems on her rented typewriter. She mailed nine poems to magazines, hoping to get them published.

Editors mailed May's poems right back. That hurt her more than hearing her new landlady say, "Clear out of here."

May moved to the worst room she'd lived in so far. She called it a "cell." Yet she had such pride that she sent back to her dad the twenty-five dollars he tried to lend her. She took a job cleaning Arnold's apartment for a few dollars a week. She walked around New York interviewing for other work. She looked like a beggar in her ragged dress.

Finally she broke down and went to the relief office. (Welfare was known as "relief " in those days.) May told the relief officer that she'd gradually run out of clothes since arriving in New York. She asked for money enough to buy a coat, shoes, and a hat. Buying was better than shoplifting again. She'd done that to get the dress she'd worn to the relief office! She'd gone to Klein's Department Store, tried on a dress, and worn it under her old dress when leaving the store.

Friends had explained to May that in order to get relief money she couldn't have parents who were willing to support her. So May told the relief officer that she wasn't in touch with her parents. May said she didn't know if they were alive or dead. On the papers she filled out May named her aunt Marie as her only living relative.

In her new clothes May stood in picket lines with others who needed jobs. Anzia had urged May to demonstrate, to show the United States government that writers, too, needed to be given jobs during the Great

Depression. May made friends with union members. They wanted her to join them in the Workers Alliance, Local 87.

"Joining a union is too much like getting religion," May told them. She'd rather have stayed aloof from the organization—from membership in any crowd of like-minded people. But she joined anyway. She made union friends and wrote articles for their newsletter. For fun she wrote a play to be presented at a union meeting.

The first scene of May's play begins with a jobless man asking his wife about dinner:

Mr. H: When do we eat?

Mrs. H: You mean *what* do we eat. There isn't a thing in the house. We have five days to go on our Relief Allowance, and it's all spent but ten cents.

Later in this same play May gives poor people some silly recipes to use for dinner. Writing such humor was a way May had of cheering herself up when life seemed bleak—and of cheering others:

CREPE PAPER SALAD

Take some old colored crepe paper—
red, green, blue makes a delightful combination.
Shred thin, in the manner of coleslaw.
In place of mayonnaise, use a dab of toothpaste.
The crepe paper furnishes very good roughage.

ICICLE PARFAIT

Gather two fresh icicles and peel.
Slice them into parfait dishes.

48

Finally, in August 1938, a job found May! The United States government hired her to join hundreds of others—including Anzia—in the Federal Writers' Project. These were writers who, like May, couldn't find work during the depression. They'd all been terribly poor. Now they were being paid twenty dollars a week to collect oral histories from people throughout the United States. These were going to be published as a story of America, told by Americans themselves.

May spent hours each week interviewing people in New York, ordinary people, not stars in movies or sports. "Talk freely," May told them. She was a sympathetic listener. She wrote down every word she could and then used her memory for the rest. At home she typed the interviews without improving what she'd heard.

People told her mostly about their jobs. She listened to a former lumberjack, a marine radio operator, a clerk at Macy's department store. Sometimes May would catch workers in groups at lunch. She'd write down their conversations in the form of a play, like this one about women who were telegraph operators:

Grace: Listen, the new floorman stopped at my machine today and he says "How are you doing?" So I looks up at him, gives him the bright eye, and I says, "I could do better without you breathing down my neck."

Dot: Oh, you didn't really!

Grace: So help me, I did. If you know what I mean.

Ruth: He's fresh. I don't like his looks. Y'know how he puts his paw casually on your shoulder? Gives me the shivers.

Dot: The other floorman we had was better. Remember Bald Freddy?

Grace: I used to keep a crossword puzzle on my lap and fool with it between sending wires. Gee, one day Freddy came up behind me and he catches me and he stoops down and whispers in my ear, "A 'monkey' in three letters is 'ape.' " He meant it for an insult but I wasn't fazed. I laughed and wrote it in, right in front of his nose.

Dot: Listen to me, Grace. You watch your step. You may think it's funny but I've seen girls get the sack for a lot less than that. Never trust a supervisor. They kid you and turn in your number. Next payday you get a suspension.

Working for the Federal Writers' Project left May time to take a drawing class with the artist Hans Bohler. In class he asked his students to draw one another. May noticed her pencil would flit quickly over the paper when she'd make sketches of the thin students. She'd work slowly, her hand feeling heavy, while sketching fat students. Hans Bohler made several drawings of May and gave them to her. She wasn't sure if she liked them. She described herself as looking "desperately calm."

May could appear to be calm while she was really quite worried. Both these feelings sprang from her choice of living independently. Sure, she was free to be a writer. But she had to struggle to pay for her rent, food, and clothes. She'd been alone in the city of New York for two years now. Her parents had all but given up on her return home.

I'M ONE

I do not have.
I do not expect.
I do not owe.

I'm one,
the only one,
free in my life.

Each day perfect,
each day a thousand years.
Time is in me.

I swallow the sun.
I'm the one, the only
one in my life.

Oh, windless day
within me,
Oh, silence and sun.

6

YOU CAN'T HAVE
YOUR CAKE

*T*he lie May told in order to get her relief money came back to haunt her. She was fired from the Federal Writers' Project!

Aunt Marie played a part in this muddle. When a relief agent got in touch with her to ask if May Swenson was really an orphan, Aunt Marie blurted out that Professor Dan Arthur Swenson and his wife, Margaret, lived in Logan and May knew it.

After that, the relief agent decided that May didn't deserve money from the United States government and that her dad should be supporting her. May, of course, wouldn't take her dad's help. Hoping he'd forgive the embarrassment she'd caused him, May wrote him a long letter (dated October 8, 1940). In a straightforward way she gave details of her life since leaving Utah. She explained how hard it had been in New York to get a job and keep it. May said she didn't need help from home. In fact, she let her dad know she'd been saving money during her time with the Federal Writers' Project. She mentioned she'd been living (since 1938) with a friend who'd paid half the rent.

May closed her letter this way: "Dad, you will ask yourself why didn't I follow a more sensible path— take out teaching credits, for instance, stay at home, and perhaps I could have a secure position like Sunny has now. I wanted to be a writer. If I ever find a way, acceptable to myself, to solve the bread-and-butter question, I *will* be a writer."

May's roommate was Anca Vrbovska, a poet who'd come to New York from Czechoslovakia. Anca had left behind her mother and other relatives. Because they were Jewish, their lives were now in danger, for Nazi Germany was taking over Czechoslovakia. Jews were being treated harshly, and some were being murdered. Anca grew more worried each day about her family.

She was concerned, as well, about poor people in America's depression. She wanted the United States government to commit itself to them. Anca herself had been on relief. She'd taken part in union demonstrations such as sit-down strikes. She also belonged to the Communist party of America. Its leaders argued that wealth should be taken away from the few and divided equally among all people. Anca discussed these beliefs with May, who listened and was sympathetic to peoples' troubles but unwilling to join the Communist party.

"Party leaders are a pack of dimwits," said May. She thought the same was true of leaders—especially politicians—in general. She'd noticed that mostly the unimaginative rose to the tops of organizations.

When May wouldn't agree with Anca about politics, Anca became angry and difficult.

"Anca was a wildcat, dwelling by raging waters," May wrote. Their friendship went from peace to storm, storm to peace.

During peaceful times they played chess and listened to the radio. They discussed the poets they were reading—William Blake, John Donne, and Edgar Allan Poe. Anca introduced May to the stories of Franz Kafka, a Czech writer. They talked about their own poems and encouraged each other to keep on writing, no matter what. On weekends they hiked on Bear Mountain, walked the beach at Coney Island, and poked around Greenwich Village. They ate Chinese dinners after parties at the Artists' Gallery. They made dinner for their union friends, enough spaghetti "to stuff a mattress." They played friendly games of poker with their Greenwich Village friends.

"The light was warm and yellow in our apartment," May wrote. This was her first real home in New York. She kept a bowl of fresh fruit on the kitchen table to remind herself of Logan. She smoked a pipe in front of the fireplace. She had a frog and a salamander in a tank with mosses she'd gathered in the country.

Sometimes Anca would go into frightening rages about politics and about the world war that seemed to be coming on. She'd break the heads off chess pieces and call May "weak" and a "fence sitter." May wouldn't argue. Then Anca would call May "hypocritical" for being nice to people who weren't nice to her.

"You're still a child," Anca yelled at May.

"Well, if I am so what so what so what?" May wrote in her diary. She thought Anca had "unmanageable emotions."

May felt squelched. But her silence wasn't weakness. Inside she held on tightly to her own vision of life. She didn't want to reform the world. She said, "I only want to live in it, laugh at it, relish it. I want to paint horses, ride horses and hear music and weep and write poetry and read my own poetry out loud to myself. I want to learn to be beautiful and also to create beauty and I want my happiness no matter how little, sharp, and sweet."

These were two very different women, May and Anca, poets living together at the beginning of World War II.

They each needed a separate place to write, yet their apartment was too small for privacy. They needed time away from their jobs, yet they had to earn their rent. They needed subjects to write about, and here Anca seemed to come out ahead. She'd read more books on many more subjects. She had a better education. And she was involved in politics that "mattered," she said.

May didn't put book learning and world events into her poems of the 1940s. She wrote about her dreams of Logan:

NIGHTLY VISION

Green rivers that enwrap my home,
I see you twining still in dreams.
There is perpetual afternoon,
And summer brooding by those streams. . . .

Anca's dreams were unhappy ones. She'd learned that her brother and two cousins had been taken away to a Nazi labor camp. After that her letters from home stopped. She heard nothing more until the war ended in 1945, when a cousin's letter told her: "Dear Anca, Thy sister and her family and at last thy mother were deported. They never gave us a sign about themselves and they didn't come back. Thy mother was killed in a gas chamber. Alas! I cannot write anything cheerful."

These deaths and others became subjects for Anca's poetry. May, too, was writing about death, her own rather than other people's. May's voice is soft spoken. Anca cries out for all human beings.

GOOD LORD
by ANCA VRBOVSKA

The family gone up as smoke
through the chimneys of Auschwitz

    Good people they were
    they believed in HIM

Especially, the Mother.
Her last letter—a Credo:
      The good Lord will not forget us.
      The good Lord will not forsake us. . . .

I WILL LIE DOWN
by MAY SWENSON

I will lie down in autumn
let birds be flying

Swept into a hollow
by the wind
I'll wait for dying

I will lie inert unseen
my hair same-colored
with grass and leaves . . .

Once in a while their poems were published in *The Raven,* a small magazine put out by the Raven Poetry Circle of Greenwich Village. But usually poems were returned to them unpublished. When this happened, Anca urged May to keep writing.

"I'm no poet," May would answer.

"You're a fine poet. Editors are idiots. They're fools and a plague," Anca raged.

May was also writing stories and putting herself in

them as a character. She's a timid woman who can't swim in "A Day at the Sea." In another story, she's a woman who goes to the opera wearing all the wrong clothes. May effectively told what her characters looked like, and she was good at describing the rooms they lived in and their gardens. What she could not do well was tell a story! Nothing much happens to her characters. They stare out windows and think. They lie in bed and think. They stand on the seashore and talk and talk.

In one of May's stories that *does* have a plot, a character tells his friends how to get money from the relief office. Then the check comes in the mail, and they can live in shabby comfort. But their friendship is spoiled by the differences in their personalities. May sent this story to *Story* magazine with a letter that said:

"Dear Editor, Enclosed is my story, 'You Can't Have Your Cake.' I feel sure no other magazine will have it. *Story* might like it, being the one magazine in America which does not base acceptance on the following questions: Has the author a big *name?* Is the story recommended by another writer?"

May's story was rejected. But her letter shows she'd learned two secrets of publishing: She'd learned that editors were looking for well-known writers to put in their magazines, and she'd learned that even a nobody like May Swenson had a chance of being published if an editor believed she was a friend of a famous writer.

May hadn't met any famous writers in New York. She did know a famous sculptor, Saul Baizerman. He was called "the man with the hammer." He used a hammer to pound out details on the huge statues he made. In the 1940s May attended Saul's sculpting class and became his friend. She asked him and his wife to read her poems and give her an honest opinion.

"You are helping me very, very much," May told the Baizermans. "You go into the soul of a poem. I am not always able to see in my work what is pure and what is unconsciously fake."

Anca's comments about poetry had been helpful in the past. But more and more often the two friends were at odds. Finally, in 1947, Anca crossed the Atlantic for a long stay with her one sister left alive in Czechoslovakia. May crossed the United States for a visit with her whole family.

She spent her time outdoors in Logan, hiking and horseback riding in the canyon. She helped her father in his orchard. Paul and Margaret still lived at home. Dan, George, Ruth, and Beth were married and staying in apartments in the Swenson family house. Grace had moved to Hollywood, California, where she was an actress in small parts in movies. Roy lived in Salt Lake. He offered to drive May and their dad and mother to California to see Grace.

They piled into Roy's car. They drove first through Zion Canyon and Bryce Canyon in southern Utah.

"Rocks are the colors of smouldering coals, of coral, of cream," May wrote to Anca.

California seemed peaceful to May after her eleven years in noisy, rushed New York. Californians were friendly and full of spunk, especially Grace. She had renamed herself Michael Raine.

"Grace has gone Hollywood," May noticed. "She's blonder. She's dressed to the teeth."

They drove to Santa Monica beach under a wide, brilliant sky. May remembered it when she got back to New York:

"New York is like a dark, damp underground crevice. How small, dingy, and cramped the apartment looked when I unlocked the door." May didn't stay long in that apartment. She'd made up her mind to find a more cheerful place, away from Anca.

May cleaned the old apartment. She left everything behind except a red footstool and a stack of her books and papers. She moved to a furnished room at 23 Perry Street in Greenwich Village. Her room overlooked the garden of the Church of Saint John. She shared a kitchen, living room, and bath with other renters.

May had written only fifty poems in the ten years she'd lived with Anca, a strong friend who'd taken up her free time. Now May promised herself she would live according to a pattern she cut for herself. She'd get on with her own work.

Among the first poems May wrote in her new home on Perry Street is "The Key to Everything." It tells, in May's gentle way, about a difficult, impossible friendship.

THE KEY TO EVERYTHING

Is there anything I can do
or has everything been done
or do
you prefer somebody else to do
it or don't
you trust me to do
it right or is it hopeless and no one can do
a thing or do
you suppose I don't
really want to do
it and am just saying that or don't
you hear me at all or what? . . .

If I knew what your
name was I'd
prove it's your
own name spelled backwards or
twisted in some way the one you
keep mumbling but you
won't tell me your
name or
don't you know it
yourself that's it
of course you've
forgotten or
never quite knew it or
weren't willing to believe it

Then there is something I
can do I
can find your name for you
that's the key to everything once you'd
repeat it clearly you'd
come awake you'd
get up and walk knowing where you're
going where you
came from. . . .

7

HER MANAGEMENT

*M*ay had one thousand dollars in the bank. She'd saved it from the salary she'd earned from 1942 through 1948. For those seven years she'd been an assistant to the boss of an association of druggists. She'd written speeches for him to give at meetings. She'd typed his letters and edited a weekly newsletter for the member druggists. She'd even worn the proper clothes to work, including gloves, a hat, and itchy nylon stockings, which she hated.

With her improved office skills May could look forward to a better salary from the Federal Wholesale Druggists. Or she could easily find a writing job with another big business. But rather than trying, she decided to quit working for others and live on her savings. The thousand dollars would last her a whole year, she thought. In that time she'd write poetry, write more poetry, and do whatever else it took to make a name for herself.

She bought a portable typewriter. She stayed home in her large, private room. She reread everything she'd ever written, figuring out what was good, what wasn't. She asked herself what she should write about. "What is there?" she asked.

"Only yourself within yourself," she answered.

May plunged back into her habit of automatic writing:

"I only want to hear the typewriter going this is a charming room and the windows like pictures colored pictures behind the tree branches just coming into leaf."

May told herself not to stop until her fingers got tired. Once she typed for hours until she came to this point: "What if I were to write a poem right now? Hey, little typewriter. You're my collaborator. We're going to be very fond of each other and we're going to carve a hard, tall strong, and pretty-colored totem for ourselves and anybody who cares to gape at it."

This ambition kept May going each day. Her way of working was to begin poems with lines that seemed to leap out of thin air: "feel like a bird," she scribbled in her notebook as she watched birds in a park and wondered how it would feel to have wings. At her desk she finished this poem.

feel like A Bird
understand
he has no hand

instead A Wing
close-lapped
mysterious thing . . .

hand better
than A Wing?
to gather A Heap
to clasp A Mate?

or leap
lone-free and mount
on muffled shoulders
to span A Fate?

Entire stanzas of poems would spring into May's head, not simply opening or closing lines. For example in one "gulp" she wrote her feelings of loving someone:

> I wear your smile upon my lips
> arising on mornings innocent
> Your laughter overflows my throat
> Your skin is a fleece about me
> With your princely walk I salute the sun
> People say I am handsome

The process by which words, sentences, stanzas, and entire poems spring into poets' heads is complex and not well understood, not even by poets themselves. May consciously helped herself "receive" poems by keeping her mind open to what was going on around her every moment. She watched with enjoyment things taking place right before her eyes. She wasn't constantly thinking of the past or planning the future. She carried a pad and pencil to catch her thoughts as they happened.

For May, writing was always the easy part of being a published poet. Much harder for her was asking others to help her find a publisher. May's pride stood in the way—and her timidness. She believed her poems were good. She wanted them to find a place in magazines on their own merit, not because someone spoke to an editor about how well she wrote. But now, in 1949, May dropped her pride, overcame her shyness, and asked an acquaintance, Alfred Kreymborg, to help her. She knew him from the chess club and the Raven Poetry Circle in the Village. He'd written plays, a novel, and

May at the time of her "breakthrough": having a poem accepted for publication by a national magazine

eight books of poetry. He ought to know editors who might like her style of writing, May reasoned.

"Kreymborg's a merry old rascal type," May wrote in her diary. "He's coming to see me and read to me from his work in progress."

During this meeting May followed the pattern she'd set in college. She'd always tried to help whoever helped her with her work, if only by listening to their poems being read and then saying kind words about them. She liked some of Kreymborg's poems despite thinking that they were old-fashioned. Kreymborg liked May's poems because they were "healthy" and not "negative" like so much modern poetry. He labeled her work "bold" and "original" and suggested she send poems to his editor friends. He allowed May to use his name in her letters of submission.

So May wrote, "Dear Editor: At the suggestion of Mr. Alfred Kreymborg I am submitting this group of poems." She signed her letters: "With kind regards and many thanks for your attention to my work."

And her answers? All were no, including these:

"No, we don't like them."

"No, we are filled up with poetry."

"Your poems do not meet our editorial needs at present."

"They do not come up to our standards."

"I can't find any in this group that doesn't seem to miss."

May continued to work in her silent room. She revised old poems, finished new ones, and sent batches of them to editors. These, too, were returned, but now with comments:

"There are some very good things here. But somehow these don't seem quite right for us."

"We can't use them although they arouse interest."

"This is able work."

May was getting closer to a breakthrough. She kept writing, revising, retyping, buying stamps, licking them, licking envelopes, and waiting downstairs on Perry Street for the mail carrier to come.

Weeks and months passed, and then—hurrah! An editor friend of Kreymborg's published May's poem "Haymaking" in the August 20, 1949, issue of the *Saturday Review of Literature*. He paid May twenty-five dollars for it.

May was quick to use "Haymaking" to open doors at other magazines. She wrote letters to editors saying, "You may have noticed a poem of mine in this week's *Saturday Review*." May knew that editors often judged poets by the magazines in which they were published, and *Saturday Review* was one of the best at that time.

Kreymborg's name helped May sell five poems to a newspaper in Dallas, Texas, the *Times Herald*. With part of her fifty-dollar paycheck May rushed out and bought a new pair of shoes.

As time passed she connected with editors who liked her poetry for its own sake, not just because it was pushed by others. James Laughlin, the owner of New Directions Press, told May she'd sent him some "absolutely swell poems." He accepted six of them. He was an editor who liked to discover new writers. He liked poets who had nerve enough to be original, who didn't try to imitate popular poets of the day.

Editors began to offer May advice about improving her poems. Karl Shapiro of *Poetry* magazine told her that parts of her poems were "overdone." Editor Cid Corman of *Origin* wrote to May about her "overdone descriptions," which buried her ideas away from readers. He said, "May, your language points to itself. You have a tendency toward pleasure in language for its own sake."

"Well, what if I do?" May said to herself. She loved playing with words. They were her toys, and she claimed she didn't care if her poems pleased Corman, Shapiro, or anyone else.

But she did care—at least half of her did. She was her own toughest critic and recognized her urge to overwrite. For instance, in ending her poem "Sun," she'd written (in April 1949):

> you are up afork the first ringing word
> of potent joy the sharp-tined golden shout
> divine and glistening your beard with dewy flames
> sprinting to the pantheon and your godlike games

She'd had fun choosing the adjectives to pour into "Sun," but she'd weakened the poem with too many of them. Moreover, she recognized that the poem was a description only. It had no points to make.

If she were to write stronger poems, they must be rooted in her own ideas about life. Yet she felt she hadn't devised an overall philosophy. She was still asking herself, "Who am I? What is life for? How can I find the answers to these questions?"

"I'm inclined to agree with your criticism," May replied to Cid Corman. "Thanks for it."

May asked several of her new editors, as well as Kreymborg, to write letters of recommendation for her to Yaddo, an artists' colony in Saratoga Springs, New York. Their praise helped get her invited to spend two months (in 1950) with a group of writers, painters, and composers who wanted to work on their projects in peace and quiet. At Yaddo, a large mansion with a rose garden, they each had their own work spaces. Some of these were cottages in groves of pine and oak trees. Colonists were served three meals a day, including their dinner in a large dining room that had lighted candles and high-back chairs around the long, carved table. Lunches were given out in picnic baskets. There were no chores to be done. The stay at Yaddo was free.

Unexpected things happened to May there. She caught a baby snake, purple and gray. Wandering around in the woods she walked into a bog, sank up to her knees, and was forced to step out of a shoe to get away. In the evenings she surprised herself by being sociable. She played Scrabble and Chinese checkers with others. They all gave a masquerade party, to which May went as a unicorn, wearing a silver-and-gray mask made from paper. During the evening May took off her mask and sang a song in Swedish.

At other times May felt like hiding in a corner.

"I'm not good at social chatter," she wrote in her diary. "I hold conversations with myself. I'm two eyes looking out of a suit of armor. I write because I can't talk."

When May felt secure at Yaddo she let friends there read her poems. The composer Otto Luening responded by setting "The Tiger's Ghost" to music. Later, back in New York, Otto's friendship brought about May's first meeting with a powerful editor, Howard Moss. Poets all around America wanted Howard Moss to choose their work to publish in *The New Yorker* magazine. May would send him poems she'd written at Yaddo.

Elizabeth Bishop with May in a garden at Yaddo. Their friend is artist Beauford Delaney, who drew a portrait of May in pastels as she wrote her poem "Am I Becoming?"

She believed that much of what happened to her was accidental. She spoke often of her lucky breaks, saying, for example, that her talent was only a matter of luck. She said it was pure luck she'd met Alfred Kreymborg, Otto Luening, Elizabeth Bishop, and others who later helped her career. May never bragged about the way she was managing her career as a poet. She felt that using people was "messy stuff," but she'd have to push on with it.

"Getting born is messy," she said.

The help she received seemed to her as accidental, random, and generous as the events she describes in a poem about Mother Nature, "Her Management." Here May's description is lavish but not overdone. And in this poem, May's philosophy—her acceptance of her place in nature—is not buried and hard to dig up.

HER MANAGEMENT

She does not place, relate, or name
the objects of her hall,
nor bother to repair her ceiling,
sweep her floor, or paint a wall
symmetrical with mountains.

Cylindrical, her tent
is pitched of ocean on one side
and—rakish accident—
forest on the other;
granular, her rug

of many marbles, or of roots,
or needles, or a bog—
outrageous in its pattern.
The furniture is pine
and oak and birch and beech and elm;

the water couch is fine.
Mottled clouds, and lightning rifts,
leaking stars and whole
gushing moons despoil her roof.
Contemptuous of control,

she lets a furnace burn all day,
she lets the winds be wild.
Broken, rotting, shambled things
lie where they like, are piled
on the same tables with her sweets,

her fruits, and scented stuffs.
Her management is beauty.
Of careless silks and roughs,
rumpled rocks, the straightest rain,
blizzards, roses, crows,

April lambs and graveyards,
she *chances* to compose
a rich and sloven manor.
Her prosperous tapestries
are too effusive in design

for our analyses—
we, who through her textures move,
we specks upon her glass,
who try to place, relate and name
all things within her mass.

8

THE TRUTH IS FORCED

I have steel, steel, steel in my ears all day to make a living," May would complain to anyone who asked about the full-time job she'd found after her time off to write. Now she was typing as many as sixty letters a day in the order department of a New York steel business, Frasse and Co., Inc.

During coffee breaks May's coworkers chatted about spending their salaries on clothes, hairdos, movies, and boyfriends. May didn't join in. She was pinching every penny for another year of freedom. She kept herself from being numb with boredom by sneaking a notepad from her purse and writing poems. When others left for lunch she'd stay to think about the dreams she'd had the night before. Remembering them was hard work.

She'd dreamed she should quit smoking. She'd dreamed of being fired from her job. She'd dreamed horrid things about traveling: getting lost, forgetting her suitcase and then feeling foolish.

If no one was watching her closely, May would type up her dreams. She'd use Frasse stationery. That way her dreams looked just like business letters if a boss peeked over her shoulder.

May collected her dreams in a file she labeled "Chapters of the Night." She studied them. She wanted to discover the parts of herself that were hidden when she was awake. She read books about dreaming. She discussed her dreams with friends who were going to doctors to find out what dreams meant. May couldn't afford doctors. Besides, she hated to depend on them or on anyone else. She believed she could figure herself out. Then she'd use her deeper self-understanding in poems.

At night and on weekends May would spread out all her poems on a table. She'd pick out some to send away to poetry contests. She'd arrange the ones she liked best in books that she hoped to get published. She gave her books titles: *The Green Moment, The Shadow Maker, Sky-Acquainted, Another Animal.* She used her spare time filling out applications to get a Ford Foundation grant, a Rockefeller, a Guggenheim— any one or all three would be lovely for *any* poet.

May knew it was harder for a woman poet than for a man to get a Guggenheim grant. She hoped it might help her chances to have a recommendation from a famous woman poet, Elizabeth Bishop. May dropped her pride and asked Elizabeth.

They had met at Yaddo. Since then they'd become friends by writing letters to each other. Elizabeth was an American living in Brazil. She had the leisure to be a full-time poet because she'd been given money to live on by her family. She was about May's age but already Elizabeth had published a book of poems and won prizes.

It's not easy for two poets to be friends. One reason is that they are both trying to get into the same few magazines that have space for poems. Both are also trying to get their books published by the few companies that publish poetry. Books of poetry seldom earn back the money spent to print them. That's because in the United States hardly anyone buys poetry or reads it. So poets become rivals rather than friends—rivals for readers and publishers.

Rival poets can get jealous of one another over who wins big prizes or grants and over who ends up with the best publisher and sells the most books. Such jealousy can cause nasty gossip that damages poets' lives. To get revenge, poets sometimes make "war" on one another. They write mean criticism in magazines. They see to it that their own friends win prizes, even if they don't deserve to win.

May didn't have to think twice about a friendship with Elizabeth Bishop. May loved and admired Elizabeth's poems, and that was that.

"I feel weight rather than surface when I read Elizabeth. In my own poems I'm too concerned with the skin of things, the shiney skin," May said.

Skin or not, May loved her own poems. She called them her "children," and she wasn't afraid to send them along in letters to Elizabeth Bishop. Elizabeth praised May for being "open-minded" and "unpretentious" and said May's poems were bound to improve. In some of her letters Elizabeth suggested changes that she believed would help May's poems. Certainly May paid attention to these suggestions and even more attention to Elizabeth's poems, probing them, rereading them to discover what Elizabeth was saying about life and noting her ways of saying it. But May trusted her own instincts on the poems she'd sent Elizabeth.

"I'm afraid I'm committed to it in spite of everything against it," May wrote, rejecting changes.

Their long-distance friendship was also concerned with things besides poetry. Elizabeth described her apartment in Rio de Janeiro and her house in a small mountain town. She told stories about her cook and housekeeper, her many visitors, her garden, birds, and cats.

May was entranced. Her own letters told about leaving one job in order to write in peace and then hunting for another, ending up in a "cage of work." She told news of people they'd both known at Yaddo. She told of her tussles with her landlord on Perry Street, Father Graf. He'd cut down a tree in the garden after all his renters had begged him not to.

May wrote: "Last year we had a great feud with Graf over painting our apartment, which hadn't been done for three years. Finally we agreed to his offer to paint half of it, while the other half would be done this year. This year he said he didn't remember promising anything like that but if we would give him 15% more rent we could get it painted."

In her poem "The Garden of St. John's," May flat out calls Father Graf "hard hearted." She writes of his stiff mouth saying *amens*. She goes on with her picture of Graf, but in a roundabout way, using a viper as a symbol for him:

> Two trees like swans' necks twine in the garden
>   beside the wall of St. John's in the city
> Brooding and cool in the shade of the garden
>   the scrolled beds of ivy glitter like vipers

May would rather have been living in her ideal home, the home she described in a letter to a friend: a roomy cave with a sand floor and a stone to sit on, a stream nearby to bathe in, and a fire out front for heat and light. May was almost forty years old, yet she felt as

May's terrace hung over this garden. She wrote "Yellow telephones in a row are ringing" about daffodils there.

close to nature as she had in the hay field of her childhood.

"A lion skin would be the garment for me," May wrote in 1952.

Despite the help of Elizabeth Bishop, May didn't get a Guggenheim. The closest she came to it was at a party with her art teacher, Saul Baizerman. He'd been given a three-thousand–dollar Guggenheim grant. May called it a "bundle."

She felt the chains of yet another office job tighten around her, and there were other disappointments. One by one she collected eight letters of rejection from *The New Yorker*. Each letter stung. Her books were returned by editors. She failed to win a poetry contest sponsored by Yale University. In a blue mood she laid aside the very poem she was writing. To her it "missed the mark."

She placed it in a folder she labeled "Working." Thirty other poems of hers had been sent out to editors, who were slow to answer their mail. It might take months for them to say yes or no. They sometimes lost poems in their files. But despite all that, May had learned that something good could happen at any time, as long as she had a mail carrier or a telephone! It rang one fine day and Howard Moss told May her poem "By Morning" would be used in *The New Yorker*.

> Some for everyone
>   plenty
>
>   and more coming
>
> Fresh   dainty   airily arriving
>   everywhere at once
>
> Transparent at first
>   each faint slice
>   slow   soundlessly tumbling
>
>   then quickly thickly a gracious fleece
>   will spread like youth   like wheat
>   over the city

Each building will be   a hill
  all sharps made round

  dark worn noisy narrows made still
  wide   flat   clean   spaces

Streets will be   fields
  cars be   fumbling sheep

A deep bright harvest will be seeded
  in a night

By morning we'll be   children
  feeding on manna

  a new loaf on every doorsill

May had begun the poem during a New York snowfall
and then worked on it while riding the bus to Yaddo
for her stay there in 1952. She'd managed to keep
herself from overdescribing the snow and to make it
reveal her love for calmness, stillness, and generosity.
Howard Moss thought that readers would not understand the poem's subject if the word *snow* were left
out of the title. As an editor his job was to think of his
readers. He asked May to change the title to "Snow by
Morning."

May hoped readers would work for an understanding of "By Morning." It was one of her riddle poems.
These came from her natural urge to keep secrets
and be puzzling. If she changed the title, readers
would lose the fun of discovering the snow for themselves.

But she knuckled under and changed the title. That
made her feel weak, uneasy, guilty. Yet the chance to
get into such a fine magazine seemed worth it.

Other guilts haunted May. She remembered she had

tugged at Otto Luening to help her with Howard Moss. She remembered lunches with editors when she'd tugged at them to publish her books. She'd gone to hated parties just for a chance to meet people who would then write good things about her poems. At those parties she'd listen to critics speak endlessly about what poetry should "be" or "do" or "mean" in order for it to succeed. When they asked May her rules for poetry, she wanted to tell them that as far as she was concerned there were none.

"A poem's business is to be fascinating," she'd say instead. That was bland enough not to offend anyone. She'd save the truth for her poems. "Not able to be honest in person, I wish to be honest in poetry," she wrote in "The Truth Is Forced."

> One must be honest somewhere. I wish
> to be honest in poetry.
> With the written word.
> Where I can say and cross out
> and say over and say around
> and say on top of and say in between
> and say in symbol, in riddle,
> in double meaning, under masks
> of any feature, in the skins
> of every creature.
> And in my own skin, naked.
> I am glad, indeed I dearly crave
> to become naked in poetry,
> to force the truth
> through a poem. . . .

May wrote in her diary, "Tugging is horrible to me. I've been waiting for the mailman to bring me success.

It's shameful. I'm a thousand times luckier than anyone I know. I have a nice place to live, loving parents, health. But I'm selfish and clamlike."

True, May preferred to keep to herself. But she was always willing to write letters to keep up with people. Friends, editors, and her family heard from her regularly. Her parents were in Sweden for a year as missionaries for the Mormon church. May wrote them often with good news, like the two hundred dollars she'd won from the Poetry Center. Three judges had chosen May from the fifty-three poets who'd entered that contest.

Then came wonderful news, the best of May's career so far. Her book of poems, *Another Animal,* was going to be published by Charles Scribner's Sons. She now had the same publisher as Thomas Wolfe, her favorite writer when she arrived in New York.

May's Mormon family was putting together its own book about the Swensons and their children. They asked Anna Thilda May Swenson to fill out a page about herself for this book. So, in a space on the page to list children, if any, May wrote the names of the thirty-nine poems she'd published since leaving Utah.

Later she wrote a poem about what she'd name real children if she had any.

IF I HAD CHILDREN

If I had children, I might name
them astrometeorological names:
Meridian, a girl. Zenith, a boy.
Eclipse, a pretty name for either one.
Anaximander, ancient Greek scientist
(who built a gnomon on Lacedaemon,
and with it predicted the exact date

that city would be destroyed by
earthquake). . . . Anaximander, wonderful
name for a girl. Anny could be her
nickname. Ion, short for ionosphere,
would make a graceful name for
a boy. Twins could be named after
planets: Venus and Mercury, or

Neptune and Mars. They'd adore each
other's heavenly bodies shining
upon their doubles on Earth.
And have you ever thought that, of
the Nine, only one planet is female?
Venus. Unless Earth is. So, seven
of Sun's children, it seems, are male.

But, if I had children, and grandchildren, then greatgrandchildren, myriads
of newborn moons and moonlets crowding
into the viewfinder would furnish me
names both handsome and sweet:
Phoebe, Rhea, Dione among daughters
of Saturn, with Titan and Janus the

brothers. Io, Ganymede and Callisto,
Jupiter's boys: Europa and little
Amalthea, their sisters.
On Io, most exotic of the Galilean
moons, are mapped six great-and-grand
volcanoes: Loki, Hemo, Horus, Daedalus,
Tarsis, Ra. Beauties all! But all

boys. Well, if I had children
I wouldn't fix genders or orbits, only
names for them. Wobbling Phobus,
distant child of Mars, misshapen as
a frozen potato. . . . If I had such a
lopsided moon, the name Phobus would
fit. And I'd love it just the same.

9

MY POEMS

W atch the sky and see if there's not a shooting star," May wrote to a friend when *Another Animal* was published on September 14, 1954. May was kidding. She wasn't a flashy Broadway actress or New York Yankee. It took more than a first book of poems to make a star in New York, and May knew it. She'd have to be content with just a sip of fame, the short reviews in newspapers that called her poems "accomplished," "arresting," and "original without being freakish." In the *New York Times Book Review* a poet, John Ciardi, wrote of May, "She is not a promise, but a fact. She has daring, a true feeling for the structure of the whole poem, precision of phrase, and a magic eye for the exact image."

May's book didn't win the National Book Award, for which it was nominated, but May already had something she needed as badly as fame and awards: a friendship with a warm, sympathetic person who loved her poems. This was Pearl Schwartz.

"Pearl is aware of all that goes into my work, notices what's been done and how well, and receives a thrill from my poems, as I do," May wrote about Pearl in her diary. May had been living with Pearl at 23 Perry Street for four years. Pearl had been a night attendant in a hospital's tuberculosis ward and done other kinds of humanitarian jobs. Now she worked in an office as a secretary while attending night school at Hunter College. She was an A student who planned to be a teacher.

Pearl gave a party to celebrate the publication of May's book. Over the years, Pearl gave many parties, with dancing to records, singing with a guitar, word games, fortune-telling, and chatter about books and writers. May's friends from Yaddo became Pearl's friends. Pearl loved to talk to people. She was also a good listener, quick to respond with help people needed.

"She's open and direct while I'm cautious and controlled. I beat around the bush," May wrote.

A friend who often came to their parties, the writer Dan Wakefield, described May in a more flattering way. He wrote, "May had a plain, straightforward Western manner. Her face was set with powerful, unflinching eyes. The way May looked at you, she seemed to be looking into you as well. She was one of the few people I trusted enough to show the short stories I was writing."

May and Pearl were opposites (in many ways) but equal partners who lived peacefully together, taking turns with the housework, shopping for food, cooking, and doing laundry. On their free evenings they were never stuck in front of the TV. May wouldn't have one in the house. She hated advertisements. She thought they lied about life, and lying made them enemies of her poems—of any poem that told the truth.

On weekends Pearl practiced her shorthand. May sat writing at an old trestle table that served as her desk. After lunch they took walks around New York. May noticed animals wherever she was.

Pearl Schwartz holding Thistle at a front window of 23 Perry Street in Greenwich Village, and May holding Pesky, a young mutt she didn't keep for long

"It would be fun to be a mounted policeman," she said after a parade on Fifth Avenue.

In a pet-shop window the monkeys caught May's eye. To her they were little fur-covered people with five hands, counting the tail. At the zoo she listened to Jack, the lion, greet children with his loud roar. A tiger and a lion lived together in another cage. May wrote a poem about their friendship, saying that the tiger, Ranee, is "a velvet table when she walks" and the lion, Zambesi, has a "tail balled up at the end, like a riding crop."

> they avoid each other's touch; but if, passing,
> as much as a whisker of that black-and-orange head
> grazes the lion's flank, her topaz eye narrows:
> irascibly she turns with slugger's paw
> to rake the ear of her mate.
>
> Then rampant they wrestle; rich snarls
> in coils pour from their throats and nostrils.
> Like soft boulders the bodies tumble each other down.
> Then, not bothering to rise, they lounge . . .

Animals couldn't speak for themselves and had no idea what they looked like. These were two of the many reasons they attracted May. She could read their faces and playfully make up whatever she wanted about them.

Another Animal was for sale in bookstores for $3.98. May received only twelve cents per copy, which added up to almost nothing for the few copies sold. Yet the book led to other opportunities to earn money. The Poetry Center at the YMHA offered her thirty-five dollars to read from her book on the stage there. Such readings were becoming popular with teachers and students. They attended to see "what poets look like and what they're wearing," May decided, and she wondered if people thought poets were as strange-looking as their photos in textbooks.

May was deathly afraid of reading her poems to a crowd, but as always she needed money. So she practiced reading each poem aloud many times: "I want not only to write live poems but to present them lively to other ears, like the obligation to rear children after they're born," May wrote in her diary.

Practice or not, her first public reading turned out to be the longest hour she'd ever lived. And she was badly frightened again when she read her poems for a radio program, "Poets of Tomorrow." She muffed words and whistled her *s*'s into the microphone. "That's not me," May groaned, listening to a record of herself.

Another Animal helped May win a Rockefeller Writing Fellowship of two thousand dollars. She was able to quit her office job to work full-time on a poem she'd been asked for by Doris Humphry, a dancer. The poem would be read to music while dancers performed on stage at Juilliard Concert Hall. To find out what sort of a poem to write, May made an appointment to meet Humphry. They sat together at a dim table in a tavern near Central Park. May felt "sparkless" as she tried to understand what was expected of her. "It's vague to me," May said afterward.

Usually when May picked up her pencil the words came easily, almost as if someone said them in her ear. Her pencil would move as if another hand were guiding it. But now May had to force herself to write. Slowly she produced hundreds of lines, put them aside, and stubbornly wrote others.

"This poem's a dud," she admitted at last. In the end she chose just thirty-nine lines for Humphry's "Theater Piece II," which was performed in April 1956:

> O Light that leaps
> from the eye of the sun
> to every living eye,
> dwell in us!
>
> Light, kernel of all fruits
> and seed of every flower,
> tranquil light,
> garment of the air,
> fierce light,
> costume of the flame . . .

Trying to please others, May had written a stiff, pretentious poem in a style not her own. She decided against such assignments in the future. "There's comfort in writing for oneself. There is no possible critic that way," she told friends.

The Rockefeller grant allowed May and Pearl to vacation on Martha's Vineyard, an island off Cape Cod. They could afford to eat in restaurants and go to the beach every day. Pearl kept an eye on May while May waded up to her hips in the ocean. She still couldn't swim. Mostly she lay on the beach and wrote poems. She wrote more of them in Vermont, where, for two weeks in the summer of 1957, she was the Robert Frost Fellow at the Bread Loaf Writers Conference. May went there mainly for a chance to meet editors who might want to publish her next book. Also she hoped to speak privately with Robert Frost himself. She loved the plain, everyday language of his poems about nature. She

May's too shy and scared to chat with Robert Frost (right) at a cocktail party during the Bread Loaf Writers Conference. She was the Robert Frost Fellow in 1957.

wanted to tell him so and hoped he'd give her poems a boost.

They had a brief meeting. There May sat, knee to knee with the greatest poet in America. He did the talking. May "absorbed his presence." She was struck by his handsome old face, his eyes the color of turquoise. He handed her back the copy of *Another Animal* she'd given him. "It reeks of poetry," Frost said, and stood up to leave.

May was too paralyzed to ask Frost what he meant. Naturally she wanted him to mean her poems smelled of genius. But perhaps he was really saying her poems were swollen with perfume, meaning they were over-written.

"It's possible he hadn't read my poems, just opened the book and sniffed the pages," she decided later. "If I am ever important enough as a writer to have the fellows at the foot of the ladder ask me for a little boost, I won't refuse. Even if I think their work stinks I'll give them a helping hand."

May had climbed far up the ladder. Her second book, *A Cage of Spines,* would shortly be published. She was giving readings, selling poems to magazines, and winning prizes. In these ways she made about half the money she needed to live on.

For the other half May worked afternoons at New Directions Press. Her boss there, James Laughlin, had been one of the first editors in New York to publish her poems.

May's job was to read manuscripts that came in the mail. She loved the suspense of what might pop out of each envelope she opened. Right before her eyes would be the inner lives of people she'd never met, never even heard of. She passed along the best manuscripts to Laughlin. He left them in piles and mainly ignored the notes May had written about them. Laughlin liked to discover his own writers. May would have felt useless around the office if it hadn't been her job to write letters of rejection.

To soften the hurt of rejection, May wrote kind, thoughtful words to each author. She remembered her own sad days of going unpublished. That's one reason she tried to help her own friends. She laid their manuscripts on Laughlin's desk, asking him in person to read them. In this way May recommended Anca Vrbovska's poems to Laughlin.

"Anca's not half the writer you are," he said, refusing to publish Anca.

"She's twice as good as me," May replied.

She stayed at the office to write Anca a kindly letter. At the end of it she mentioned briefly her own work: "I hope to make a really good poetry before I die," May wrote. "If I'm not too lazy and manage to educate myself better, maybe I can do it."

MY POEMS

My poems are prayers to a god
to come into being.

Some mornings I have seen his hair
flash on the horizon,

some nights I have seen his heel there
clear as the moon.

My poems pray him to be
manifest like lightning—

in one pure instant abolish
and recreate the world.

10

THE POPLAR'S SHADOW

*I*n the late 1950s, the "Beatnik" poets were riding high. They traveled around the United States reading their poems in coffee houses and bars. Thousands went to hear them shout out against wars, atomic bombs, poverty, racial prejudice, and everything else they feared and hated. They used shocking words in their poems, and seldom used rhyme or other poetic devices. This made them popular with young people, who caught on to the "Beats" without poring over them in schoolbooks.

New Directions published Lawrence Ferlinghetti, one of the Beats. Reading him made May feel old *and* old-fashioned. She'd spent all those years making friends with trees, lakes, lightning, cornfields, skies—spinning her own world in poetry. She hadn't developed fierce hatreds to write about. But now maybe she'd better start trying to be negative, she was thinking. She'd better turn completely around and protest against life at the top of her voice.

> To be beat or not
> to be beat—that
> is the question

May wrote that knowing full well she couldn't be mad at the world if she tried. She had to remain her natural self. She wouldn't change the ending of so much as one poem, even to please her editor, Howard Moss.

He'd written to her about publishing "The Centaur." He'd said, "The last two stanzas of 'The Centaur' strike us as a bit too self-conscious and we'd like to cut them, if you agree."

May sent back an answer the day she got his letter: "I do balk at cutting the ending because I think the picture of the child is then left too vague. I want it known that the child is a girl. She's being scolded for acting too boyish instead of staying in the house and being a 'lady.'"

May wouldn't let her poem be ruined just so that she could see it in *The New Yorker*. She published it elsewhere.

But she did change something about herself. She changed her age after a publisher misprinted her birth date as May 28, 1919 (instead of 1913). The misprint started her thinking about really being six years younger. What if she were in her thirties, not in her forties?

For one thing there would be more office jobs open to her, jobs advertised for younger women. And, for poetry contests and grants, May would be a "younger poet." She'd appear to have come a long way in a shorter time if she could erase those years in the middle 1940s. Back then she'd written only a handful of not-very-good poems. In the ten years since, she'd been a whirlwind. She'd published nearly one hundred poems.

May didn't correct the printing error. It was picked up and used over and over. She began writing her birth year as 1919 on applications, including those for grants.

"I have done the disgusting thing of docking my age," May told her diary.

Pearl and other friends knew May's real age, but they didn't laugh at her lie. They understood it because they'd impersonated younger women themselves in order to get jobs. May was embarrassed despite their understanding. She asked Betty Kray at the Poetry Center to introduce her as an "older younger poet" or a "younger older poet."

Betty suggested that May earn money by going on a poetry tour of colleges in California. She offered to coach May to improve her reading and also to help May find the right clothes for the trip. Pearl volunteered to go along. She'd graduated from Hunter College and had time away from her job as a social worker. They'd travel together on the bus—the "good Gray Hound," May called it. Going back east after the tour, they'd stop in Logan, Utah.

Although she was "scared spitless," May's readings in San Francisco and Berkeley were less dreadful than she'd predicted. When the microphone broke down, she raised her voice. When a tall podium on stage hid her completely from sight, she sat down at a table near the audience and read from there. Then, in Logan, nothing at all went wrong! May was hailed as a celebrity, the town's first star poet. She had the time of her life presenting her poems on the Utah State campus.

Her former teacher, Dr. Pederson, introduced her to the crowd of Swensons, students, townspeople, and friends. May thanked him for teaching her that writing could be a whole life's work. Then she read some "Logan" poems, including "The Poplar's Shadow," about a tree in her home's front yard, a tree that had predicted she'd grow up to be a writer:

> When I was little, when
> the poplar was in leaf,
> its shadow made a sheaf,
> the quill of a great pen
> dark upon the lawn
> where I used to play. . . .

May's mother was on edge while May was at home. She asked May and Pearl not to smoke in public. She wanted people to think May was still a faithful Mormon. May dutifully went to church with her parents, and she pleased them in other ways. She won the Utah State slogan contest with her slogan "The campus in a canyon's lap." Then, back in New York, she found out she'd won a Guggenheim grant. She wrote immediately to her mother: "Mom, you must be praying extra hard for me because I have some good news that puts my former good fortune in the shade: a grant of $3,500.00—more than I'd ever expected in one chunk."

May had been applying for a Guggenheim for six straight years. Winning it made her feel she'd been recognized as a poet. Her friends phoned to congratulate her. She let them know her plans for spending part of the money: She'd soon be off on a trip, for she'd also won an Amy Lowell Traveling Scholarship of two thousand dollars. In order to keep that money, May had to promise to travel outside the United States.

She wanted to go to South America, to see "raw land,

unshaped by people." In such a place her sensations would be fresh for poems. Brazil was her first choice. There she'd see jungle birds and animals, and she could visit Elizabeth Bishop in the mountains.

Pearl thought they should drive through Europe, stopping at sights she'd seen in pictures all her life. She looked forward to using the Spanish and Italian she'd learned in classes. Her plan was to take a tent and sleeping bags to save money by camping instead of going to hotels all the time. May agreed. She'd buy the car if Pearl would drive it in Europe. May still had no driver's license.

"I'll look for the unnoticed and unfound in Europe," May promised herself.

She felt pushed "like a piece of ice in an iceflow" before leaving. There was so much to do, and meanwhile the landlord, Father Graf, was hounding her again. "There's no satisfying a woman tenant," he concluded when he got nowhere with May. She had to spend time fighting him at the rent-control board or he would have raised the rent sharply. She also took French lessons and attended farewell parties given for her. She was as uncomfortable as ever in rooms full of "smeary gossip" about other writers. She wouldn't pass it on.

"Someone has to listen," May would say about her silence.

In the spring of 1960, May and Pearl sailed for France aboard the *Maasdam*. May used picture postcards to keep a record of what she saw each day, starting with the icy water in the fountains of Paris. From there on, May described dozens of fountains. She added some made-up fountains and blended them into a poem that looks like water falling on a page:

Beards of water
some of them have.
Others are blowing whistles of water.
Faces astonished that constant water
jumps from their mouths.
Jaws of lions are snarling water
through green teeth over chins of moss.
Dolphins toss jets of water
from open snouts
to an upper theatre of water.
Children are riding swans and water
coils from the S-shaped necks and spills
in flat foils from pincered bills.
A solemn curly headed bull
puts out a swollen tongue of water. . . .

In Spain they went to bullfights. They saw six bulls killed in two hours and dragged away to the sound of sleigh bells. May called it a "shabby affair," but went again when they reached the south of France. There women tossed their shoes into the bullring and men tossed their hats for the bullfighters to throw back. In Arles, France, May and Pearl waited in their seats four long, hot hours. They poured water on their heads, trying to stay cool until the fights began. They'd made the mistake of buying tickets on the sunny side of the arena.

It was worth the heat, for just as the bull entered, so did the great painter Pablo Picasso. He took a shady seat across from them. He wore a pink-striped shirt, black tie, eggshell white suit, and sombrero.

"Very quiet and impressive," May wrote on a post-card.

While camping, May and Pearl often had to fight off swarms of gnats and mosquitoes. Their tent blew down in windstorms and their air mattresses sank in heavy

May used this fountain in Rome, along with others in Italy, France, and Spain, for her poem "Fountains of Aix." In another poem she wrote, "Lombardy, Tuscany, Umbria, Calabria" three times. She loved the sound of the words.

rains. Water also brought this playful news headline from May's pen:

> FREAK DEATH OF POET
> ELECTROCUTED IN SHOWER
> OF CAMP AT AIX-EN-PROVENCE
> FOUND BEHIND LOCKED DOOR

May had been taking a shower in camp. To release the water she'd pulled a chain and was suddenly knocked screaming to the floor. She managed to get dressed and back to her tent. Later she learned the wires from an electric light had touched the water chain. Two hundred and ten volts had passed through

May's body. She was lucky: Her only injury was a fingernail that turned black.

Peach orchards and olive groves were May's favorite campsites. There she'd wake up to the hiss of leaves. At night she'd hear owls. One morning in Italy she heard bells competing with one another from many towers. At a beach camp on the Mediterranean Sea she almost learned to swim.

"The beach is level, the sea smooth and buoyant. Wouldn't it be odd if I did learn to swim at my age?"

But as always, May was happiest when writing. She'd set up her typewriter on the camp table or on her knees. She'd work for several hours a day.

"Very happy," she wrote on a postcard. Vivacious Pearl made friends wherever they drove. May made poems like this one from Florence, Italy. She'd been watching a boy who was touching Michelangelo's statue of David. May puts her own thoughts into the boy's head.

A BOY LOOKING AT BIG DAVID

I'm touching his toe.
I know I'll be brave after this.
His toenail wide as my hand,
I have to stand tall to reach it.

The big loose hand with the rock in it
by his thigh
is high above my head. The vein
from wrist to thumb, a blue strain in the marble.

As if it had natural anatomy all its own
inside it.
Somebody skinned off the top stone,
and there He stands.

I'd like to climb up there on that slippery Hip,
shinny up to the Shoulder
the other side of that thumping Neck,
and lie in the ledge on the collar-bone,

by the sling.
In that cool place
I'd stare-worship that big, full-lipped,
frown-browned, far-eyed, I-dare-you-Face.

I'd like to live on that David for a while,
get to know
how to be immortal like Him.
But I can only reach his Toe—

broad, poking over the edge of the stand.
So cool . . .
Maybe, marble Him,
he likes the warm of my hand?

11

TO MAKE A PLAY

I miss you very much, May. No one is as efficient as you in writing nice sympathetic letters to young hopefuls."

James Laughlin wrote that to May while she was in Europe. She returned to continue reading manuscripts for him at New Directions, except now she'd often ask for leave without pay to work on her own projects.

May was approaching the time when her poems alone would support her. Not that she'd found a magic recipe for writing what people would rush to buy in bookstores. May's second book hadn't sold any better than her first despite praise to the skies from critics. They'd written of May's sense of being at home with nature, her delight in the charm of all things under her gaze. Their raves brought May an invitation to teach full-time at Smith College in Massachusetts.

"I'm poorly educated myself," May gave as her excuse not to teach. She was willing to do only a reading at Smith, where she was introduced as "the poet who remembers being a horse as a girl."

"Readings are a challenge to the introvert in me," May confessed to her audiences.

If only she could have relaxed and had fun. Other poets loved being on a platform. They'd get carried away by flattery, keep reading and reading and signing autographs for hours. May had to push herself to mingle and make small talk. She'd come back to Perry Street from Wellesley, Bennington, Trinity, Dartmouth, and she'd remain upset for days.

"I don't feel well today," she says in a prosy poem, "Thursday Thoughts of a Poet," which she began after a reading:

The reason I don't feel well is that I got no sleep last night.
    I had to read my poems to students at a college
    and the next day my routine was upset
    because my mind was upset
    by too many recollections of what I should have said,
                         and didn't,
    by too many questions asked me about my poetic method. . . .

May had tried to answer students' questions honestly. She didn't pretend she had a cookie cutter that students could grab for their own poems. "There are many ways to make a poem. Ways I can do it right and ways others do it right," she'd say in a halting voice.

"I let it happen to me," she'd continue. "It sounds mysterious. It just comes to me. I never know what I'm doing or what I'm going to do. I start with an emotional jolt. All of a sudden a line comes into my head. I don't decide I'm going to do this and then that. The poem sort of begins to write itself and I see what it is making and I help it get finished. I'm often surprised at what gets made."

May was more specific when she introduced each poem at her readings. For example, she'd say she got the ideas for "Southbound on the Freeway" while riding in a car on the Garden State Parkway. She'd tried to imagine herself as a space traveler looking down at the heavy traffic. She'd mention that "Southbound" was becoming her best-known poem because it was re-printed in many schoolbooks.

SOUTHBOUND ON THE FREEWAY

A tourist came in from Orbitville,
parked in the air, and said:

The creatures of this star
are made of metal and glass.

Through the transparent parts
you can see their guts.

Their feet are round and roll
on diagrams—or long

measuring tapes—dark
with white lines.

They have four eyes.
The two in the back are red.

Sometimes you can see a 5-eyed
one, with a red eye turning

on the top of his head.
He must be special—

the others respect him,
and go slow,

when he passes, winding
among them from behind.

They all hiss as they glide,
like inches, down the marked

tapes. Those soft shapes,
shadowy inside

the hard bodies—are they
their guts or their brains?

No matter how many readings May gave, she couldn't learn to enjoy them. But she did know how to have fun with the money she'd earned by being "upset." It went straight into her savings account, where it was growing into a "large chunk" May planned as a gift to her parents in 1962.

May still remembered their twenty-fifth anniversary, which had come at the end of her first year in New York. She'd been too poor to send them a present. She couldn't afford even a phone call. All she could do was write to them saying, "How I wish I could have made a great deal of money so that you could now have a permanent vacation from the toil of so many years. Well, someday maybe."

One thousand dollars was a "great deal" of money for May in 1962. It hadn't been long since she'd lived on that amount for an entire year. Now she flew to Utah and handed her parents a thousand-dollar bill and a poem for their fiftieth anniversary:

There is only ONE bill
like this, with the
number B00068919A on it,
in the world—
and there is only ONE
Mother and ONE Father
like you in all the world—
and ONE day like this
to mark a half a hundred
years of love—

the love that made me
and my 9 brothers and
sisters— ...

May gave money to her parents—and to others—knowing that her poems would make more. Her third book, *To Mix with Time,* was selling better than Scribner's had expected. Her poems had made friends with poets. Each day the mail carrier brought May their good comments. For example, Anne Sexton wrote, "May, I am one of your fans. There are few poets writing today with all your verve, originality, sense of detail and sense of rhythm."

Josephine Jacobsen wrote, "Your poems are vivid, intelligent, strong."

Peter Davison wrote to May about her "staggering poetic equipment." He would become the editor of May's tenth book. By then she'd be an older middle-aged poet.

At the moment May was fifty. *Really* fifty in 1963, and for her the best thing about being a writer was the writing itself. May felt happiest when alone with a pad of paper on her knees and her pen racing across it. She wrote twenty-nine poems in her fiftieth year. She was about to win a theater-associate grant from the Ford Foundation—money to quit her job, maybe for good—and write a play that would be produced at the American Place Theatre in New York.

At her desk she was trying to decide on the action for her play. She thought she might write about flying. She flew so often in her dreams. She'd stand on top of a peak of summer sunshine, overlooking houses and yards in a Utah valley. She'd step off, let go, trust the air to be buoyant. All her muscles would feel nimble as fins or wings. She'd dip, rise, wheel, glide, spiral, dive up or down or merely coast, spread out or dart or fall recklessly, then catch herself and climb again, using all the power of lungs and limbs, climbing, feeling all the completeness of release and trust of letting go.

Like writing poems.

TO MAKE A PLAY

To make a play
is to make people,
to make people do
what you say;

to make real people
do and say
what you make;
to make people make

what you say real;
to make real
people make up
and do what you

make up. What you
make makes people
come and see
what people do

and say, and then
go away and do
what they see—
and see what

they do. Real
people do and say,
and you see and
make up people;

people come to see
what you do.
They see what they
do, and they

may go away undone.
You can make
people, or you
can unmake. You

can do or you
can undo. People
you make up make up
and make people;

people come to
see—to see
themselves real,
and they go away

and do what you
say—as if they
were made up,
and wore makeup.

To make a play
is to make
people; to make
people make

themselves; to
make people
make themselves
new. So real.

AFTERWORD

When May Swenson died on December 4, 1989, she left me her poems. Her last will and testament named me the executor of her literary estate, with the immediate job of putting her literary papers in order and sending them to the special collections of modern poets at the library of Washington University.

May's literary papers filled drawers, shelves, cupboards, and a closet in our house in Sea Cliff, New York, where May and I had been living for twenty-three years. I went slowly through these hundreds of files, finding draft after draft of May's published poems, stories, and articles. I also found drafts of unpublished stories, novels, plays, and several hundred unpublished poems. I found hundreds of letters May had received and copies of thousands more she'd written and sent. I found a collection of the dreams May had written down the mornings after she'd had them. I found diaries that covered fifty-three years of her life. (Her earliest diaries were lost when she'd moved from Utah to New York, leaving behind her childhood desk and all it contained.)

Over the next year I read every word on every piece of paper. I read and reread May's poems. In the time

I'd known her she'd been a famous writer whose poems appeared regularly in my favorite magazines. Every day she'd received fan mail from around the world. Now I was learning details of her early years, when she had struggled to write and be noticed.

Of course May had told me about her youth, especially about her parents' faithfulness to the Mormon church and to their large family. She'd described her dad's garden, his orchard and honeybees. She'd told me about her hard years of scrambling to earn a living in New York. With May I'd visited her mother in Logan and her brothers and sisters living in Utah. I'd met her college friend, Veneta Nielsen. In New York I'd met May's first editors: Laughlin, Ciardi, Moss. And I knew Pearl Schwartz from times I'd spend with her and May.

The Wonderful Pen of May Swenson springs from May's own words about herself, from her friends' and editors' words, and from my daily observation of her during our years together. I believe I've caught May's character in these chapters, leaving me only to say that her poems will make happier anyone who reads them. She is buried on College Hill in Logan, Utah, with a marble bench placed on the grave. Her poem "The Exchange" is carved on the bench's seat.

THE EXCHANGE

Now my body flat,
the ground breathes.
I'll be the grass.

Populous and mixed is mind.
Earth, take thought.
My mouth, be moss.

Field, go walking.
I a disk
will look down with seeming eye.

I will be time
and study to be evening.
You world, be clock.

I will stand,
a tree here,
never to know another spot.

Wind, be motion.
Birds, be passion.
Water, invite me to your bed.

On the bench's pedestal are carved these words from
her poem "The Wonderful Pen":
"Read me. Read my mind."

BOOKS BY MAY SWENSON

Another Animal (1954)

A Cage of Spines (1958)

To Mix with Time (1963)

Poems to Solve (1966)

Half Sun Half Sleep (1967)

Iconographs (1970)

More Poems to Solve (1971)

Windows & Stones (1972)
(translated from Tomas Tranströmer)

The Guess and Spell Coloring Book (1976)

New & Selected Things Taking Place (1978)

In Other Words (1987)

The Love Poems of May Swenson (1991)

The Complete Poems to Solve (1993)

Nature (1993)

INDEX